MILAN

CITY GUIDE *for* DESIGN LOVERS

The Travel Colours City Guides are for design-loving travellers who like to explore the trendiest places in each city, for travellers who see themselves as trendsetters. Each City Guide features a curated selection of the best places to "sleep, eat, drink, shop and explore", all of which have been personally tried and tested.

Edition ONE | 2019/2020

EDITOR IN CHIEF
STEFANIE FRIESE

PHOTOGRAPHY BY
FLAVIA RENZ

WORDS BY
HANNI HEINRICH

TRENDSCOUT
BIANCA FIORENTINI

PUBLISHED BY
FRIESE MEDIA GMBH, 2019
1ST EDITION - JULY 2019

PRINTED AND BOUND BY
HARTMANNDRUCK & MEDIEN GMBH IN
GERMANY ON FSC CERTIFIED UNCOATED
PAPER

ISBN   978-3-9819822-8-2

SAY HELLO

GENERAL ENQUIRIES: hello@travelcolours.de
DISTRIBUTION: sales@travelcolours.de

GET THE BOOKS ONLINE AT
www.travelcolours.guide

WE TAKE CARE

OF YOU AND OF MOTHER EARTH

We work closely with a family-run printing company that has been printing climate-neutral for years together with ClimatePartner. All our books are printed exclusively on FSC-certified paper.

STEFANIE FRIESE

It has to be nice and a bit different. The desire for lifestyle and design is always guaranteed. As the founder of Travel Colours, Stefanie is always in search of the most beautiful places.

BIANCA FIORENTINI

Lively, and always styled to perfection, Bianca is a true Milanese. Besides being a trend scout, she travels the world to hunt for interior artisanal items for her E-commerce business.

FLAVIA RENZ

Being based in Berlin, Flavia loves to keep herself surrounded by all that is beautiful and yummy. You usually find her standing on any furniture available, just to get that picture framed perfectly.

HANNI HEINRICH

As a writer, Hanni is inspired by people, human behaviour and beaches. Her favourite body lotion is sun blocker factor 50. Born in Merseburg, Germany, she is currently based in Cape Town.

SLEEP   13

EAT   43

DRINK   135

SHOP   149

EXPLORE   177

LOVE LETTER

Lately, the Italian design capital has been mentioned with the word "renaissance", describing a shift. Milan is more than a Fashion and Design destination. It is the "place to be" for the European culinary scene. Besides the classical trattoria (serving spaghetti and '80s salads), Milan offers a selection of sophisticated dining locations, always ready to host stylish guests during Fashion Week. In every way, Milan is not afraid to experiment, and while the city has certainly embraced each and every food trend, from ethnic hybridization to the brunch and gourmet fast-food obsessions, it never lost sight of its original vocation for great, timeless cuisine. That's why the Milanese restaurant scene can be relied on for the three major ingredients: tradition, innovation and nobility.

Milan is the home of world-renowned brands like Prada, Armani and Versace, and today this legacy goes further. Modern architectural projects have transformed the cityscape with a contemporary touch. Considering that 2019 marks 500 years since the death of Leonardo da Vinci, there has never been a better time to visit this Northern Italy metropolis.

Stefanie Friese

EDITOR IN CHIEF

SLEEP

THE SENATO HOTEL   15

LOCANDA PANDENUS   19

ROOM MATE BY GIULIA   23

HOTEL VIU   27

PALAZZO SEGRETI   31

THE STRAF   35

THE SISTER HOTEL   39

THE SENATO HOTEL

SLEEK BOUTIQUE HOTEL

This beautiful hotel is right in the city center, close to important attractions like the opera house La Scala and one of the city's most upmarket shopping streets. Black, white and gold dominate the interior. The reception hall radiates glamour, as does the hallway to the rooms - it visually showcases the hotel's ideas and inspirations. It also displays the story of its owners through a selection of drawings, magazine covers and maps that shed light on the city's history and its creative spirit. Senato's own brand newspaper takes everyone on a Milanese adventure filled with personalities and their passions. After all, outside the walls of this hotel the city of Milan awaits.

Via Senato 22, 20121 Milano
www.senatohotelmilano.it

LOCANDA PANDENUS

INTIMATE BOUTIQUE HOTEL

In the artistic district Brera, above a bustling cafe, art-deco fans will be delighted to see this boutique hotel. With only four rooms, the atmosphere is particularly discreet. Locanda Pandenus is sophisticated and fashionably elegant, echoing the creative chic of Milan. The rooms are refined, cosy and stylish. Antique wooden flooring has been painted black to lend a sleek elegant design, and leather stools, marble tables and brass light fixtures warm up the Art deco ambiance. The downstairs bistro happens to be one of Milan's most popular spots for brunch and aperitive.

www.pandenus.it

ROOM MATE BY GIULIA

LIVELY DESIGN HOTEL

Only a stone's throw away from Milan's Cathedral is this quirky and colourful hotel. Award-winning architect and designer Patricia Urqiuola has created a happy and fun atmosphere. There is a total of 85 rooms that refer to typical Italian domestic spaces with a vintage touch, so that guests feel like they are in a familiar setting. The fresh and lively lobby area has an eclectic mix of retro armchairs, sofas and tables in bold bright colours. Additionally, breakfast is served until noon, and guests can use a portable Wi-Fi device (called WiMate) on the go in the city.

Via Silvio Pellico 4, 20121 Milano
www.room-matehotels.com/en/giulia

HOTEL VIU

CONTEMPORARY LUXURY HOTEL

This five-star hotel is located in Porta Volta, one of Milan's most pulse-quickening districts, thanks to an influx of hip bars and restaurants. Across the road from the hotel is the Cimitero Monumentale, an impressive 19th century cemetery, which is home to elaborate tombs, sculptures and funeral shrines.

VIU is a large hotel. And functional. Capturing the zeitgeist of the modern city, with its progressive and sustainable architectural concept, this hotel honours the classic aesthetics of Milanese design with its sleek interiors. The crowning glory of Hotel VIU Milan is the VIU Terrace - the only hotel rooftop in Milan with an outdoor swimming pool that features stunning 360-degree views of the city skyline.

Via Aristotile Fioravanti 6, 20154 Milano
www.hotelviumilan.com

PALAZZO SEGRETI

HISTORIC BOUTIQUE HOTEL

This historic boutique hotel is nestled in the heart of Milan - between La Scala and Castello Sforzesco - and combines the charm of a Milanese palazzo with stylish modern design. Segreti means 'secret' in Italian, and this is exactly how the hotel feels — unassuming from the outside, it reveals one secret after another, as one makes their way through it. The rooms are all individually decorated, with different details and colour schemes. Some have floors made of reclaimed wood or resin, others with exposed brick walls and four-poster beds. However, this Palazzo creates a home that wants to seduce. For mid or long-term guests, Palazzo Segreti also offers apartments in Porta Nuova, one of the main business districts of Europe.

Via San Tomaso 8, 20121 Milano
www.palazzosegreti.com

THE STRAF

LUXURY HOTEL IN MILAN'S CENTRE

Tucked away on a quiet side street, right off Piazza del Duomo, and only a few steps away from the Cathedral and La Scala Opera House, lies the Straf Hotel. Minimalist and for the style conscious. The interior features bare cement walls, oxidised brass and black slate fittings, while cement is combined with burnished brass to create an atmosphere of warmth. Funky objects and recycled artwork, such as a pink fibreglass panel incorporating used optical lenses, decorate the walls. This adds a careful splash of colour. The hotel bar is the perfect choice for an all-day-long light lunch and happy-hour showcases various DJs.

Via S. Raffaele 3, 20121 Milano
www.straf.it

THE SISTER HOTEL

INSIDE AN ANCIENT CONVENT

This gem is secretly located behind a large gate in Via Scaldasole. The patio features old-fashioned balconies and large, arched openings from the original Sixteenth-century building, once an ancient monastery. With its nine rooms the Sister Hotel is a homage to Milan, using the typical colours of the city: black, coral red and gold. Conceived as a hub of creative ideas, this hotel belongs to the holistic container Six. Here, the architectural design and furnishings, partly vintage and partly new, are the result of the work of the designers Quincoces-Dragò, head of the Six Gallery. The food and drinks are made by the Gin012/Sixième bistro.

Via Scaldasole, 7, 20123 Milano
www.thesisterhotel.com

EAT

WITH COFFEE

THE BOTANICAL CLUB   45

LA LATTERIA   49

LÙBAR   53

oTTo   57

GOD SAVE THE FOOD   61

MARCHESI 1824   65

TENOHA   67

PLATO CHIC SUPERFOOD   71

DE SANTIS   75

GIACOMO ROSTICCERIA   77

THE BOTANICAL CLUB

ITALY'S FIRST MICRO GIN DISTILLERY

In the heart of Milan's fashion district, close to the Armani Silos, is a special place - which appears to be both a cocktail bar and a restaurant. In fact, this is Italy's first micro gin distillery, The Botanical Club. It now has three branches, and here in Tortona, it turns into a catwalk (especially over lunchtime). Big brands have their showrooms nearby and of course, the elegant fashion audience needs elegant food. The menu is fun and creative and the portions not too big. The chefs work every day to create a unique eating experience, where the most contemporary food culture goes hand in hand with the new wave of spirits.

Via Tortona, 33, 20144 Milano
www.thebotanicalclub.com

LA LATTERIA

PURE ITALIAN

Those who don't have an Italian grandmother must visit this bustling restaurant. It is located on Via San Marco in the artistic heart of Milan La Brera. La Latteria's menu changes daily - serving traditional homemade Milanese dishes, depending on what's in season. From soft buffalo mozzarella, to Gnocchi with meat ragu, to Bistecca di roast beef - this restaurant is spreading Italian love through food. Signora Maria meets the guests personally, while her husband Chef Arturo Maggi cooks all the dishes. His secret ingredient: Passion. The tables are quickly filled in this simply-decorated restaurant with that family feeling. No bookings. No credit cards. Pure Italian culinary experience.

Via S. Marco 24, 20121 Milano

LÙBAR

TASTE OF SICILY

Once upon a time, three brothers had an idea. Lucilla, Lucrezia and Ludovico founded LùBar, evolving it from street food into catering, from beach to cafeteria, from kiosk to restaurant. Today this beautiful Versaille-like restaurant is located close to the Galleria d'Arte Moderna, in Via Palestro. Pastel-coloured seats and walls emphasize the feel of the peaches-and-cream toned 17th-century. The menu is elaborate, neat and as stylish as everything else at LùBar. The cakes match the colour of the plate, the drinks match the flower decor. Besides being a restaurant, LùBar also offers food trucks, catering and party delivery.

Via Palestro 16, 20121 Milano
www.lubar.it

oTTo

A PLACE TO RELAX

Order drinks and find a comfy spot on one of the benches, under leafy branches. Or get a coffee and sit at an old school desk. oTTo, airy and bright, with green walls, is located in Paolo Sarpi, the china-town of Milan. Perfect for meeting friends, reading the newspaper or enjoy a great cocktail in the evening. The tables and chairs are jumbled - from the rattan armchair to the child's school chair, from the wooden to the metal table. Besides classical Italian coffees, this bar offers breakfast, lunches, aperitifs and dinners. oTTo is open from morning to late at night.

Via Paolo Sarpi 8, 20154 Milano
www.sarpiotto.com

GOD SAVE THE FOOD

BRUNCHES AND APERITIVE

In the heart of Milan's hipster and design district Brera, is one of the three God Save the Food. Here, directly located on the Piazza del Carmine, surrounded by Milan's prettiest church, this bar will satisfy a wide range of gastronomic cravings. No wonder this spot is a meeting point for those enjoying brunches and aperitive. From superfood salads to fajitas and fresh smoothies, God Save The Food is the remedy after a big night. The center point of God Save the Food is the open kitchen. The atmosphere changes in the evening, when the lights are dimmed, and the colorful cocktails replace the creamy cappuccinos.

Piazza del Carmine 1, 20121 Milano
www.godsavethefood.it

MARCHESI 1824

EXCELLENCE IN PASTRY AND CHOCOLATE

Marchesi 1824 is one of the oldest and most renowned patisseries in Milan - staying true to its history and tradition. Almost 200 years after the opening of this historical pastry shop in Via Santa Maria alla Porta, it is still buzzing and operates from the same address, with the same passion. Today, the shop is under the guidance of Angelo Marchesi's grandson and his family. It has become the favourite destination for elegant and cosmopolitan visitors; a mandatory destination in Milan. Now there are three branches. To this day, Marchesi stands for excellence in pastry and chocolate, and for its Panettone, the typical Milanese dessert.

Via Monte Napoleone, 9, 20121 Milano
www.pasticceriamarchesi.com

TENOHA

JAPANESE CULINARY DELICACIES

Not far from the Armani Silos, in the heart of the city, is Tenoha, where Japan meets Milan. Here guests will find a mix of aesthetic minimalism and Japanese spirit in the city. The restaurant is a fusion between bar, cafeteria and outdoor area. Around 130 seats are ready for those who come to enjoy every situation - from lunch to aperitifs, to parties. New synergies and collaborations are possible here. Tenoha offers Japanese culinary delicacies using fresh and seasonal ingredients combined with Italian customs and traditions - a unique experience surrounded by a modern atmosphere.

Via Vigevano 18, 20144 Milano
www.tenoha.it

PLATO CHIC SUPERFOOD

RICH IN NUTRITIONAL TREASURES

Inspired by 18th century Italian classical architecture, and embellished with iconic wall designs, Plato Chic Superfood welcomes everyone, from lunch to dinner time, with their innovative dishes based on superfoods rich in vitamins, antioxidants and minerals. Whether lactose- or gluten intolerant, finding healthy, healing and nourishing food at Plato Chic Superfood is easy, even for vegans. Those with fewer dietary restrictions, but who love creativity, will enjoy this too. At Plato Chic Superfood the Italian traditional cuisine becomes Super, thanks to the use of superfoods and innovative cooking techniques.

Via Cesare Battisti 6, 20122 Milano
www.platomilano.com

DE SANTIS

BELOVED PANINI SHOP

Heaven for Panini lovers, De Santis is an institution in Milan. Nestled at the Corso Magenta, this sandwich shop presents over two hundred recipes, with high quality ingredients and many homemade products, all enriching the Panini experience. De Santis offers smoked salmon, shrimps, smoked mackerel - in innovative and liberal combinations - with strong flavoured cheeses, like gorgonzola or fontina, or sometimes dressing everything with a Vodka drop. De Santis interior is simple and welcoming. Perfect for innovative Paninis in Milan.

Corso Magenta 9, 20123 Milano
www.paninidesantis.it

GIACOMO ROSTICCERIA

HOMEMADE DELICACIES

One street, five restaurants bear the same name: Giacomo. Everyone knows Giacomo and the Rosticceria is one restaurant of Giacomo's gastronomic empire. Known for exquisite roasted chicken, a lavish glass counter at the entrance welcomes everyone with a range of homemade delicacies. Many Milanese buy food here at Giacomo's Rosticceria. For take-away or for sitting-down, this restaurant is cozy, with green walls and traditional tiles. The outside is adorned with vines. If one is planning a romantic lunch, ask for a small table on the balcony. No better place to appreciate the atmosphere of intimacy and sophistication.

Via Pasquale Sottocorno 36, 20129 Milano
www.giacomomilano.com

EAT

WITH WINE

GINO12/SIXIÈME BISTROT	83
POTAFIORI	87
THE MANZONI	91
ROVELLO 18	95
28 POSTI	99
CARLO E CAMILLA IN SEGHERIA	103
AL CORTILE	107
NEBBIA	111
VÒCE AIMO E NADIA	115
SAN MAURÍ BISTROT	119
PACIFICO	123
DROGHERIA MILANESE	127
DA ZERO	131

GINO12/SIXIÈME BISTROT

CREATIVE ANTIPASTI

Nestled in the bustling Navigli district in Zona Tortona, this location offers a hidden gem in a courtyard filled with tropical plants. Once a monastery in the 16th century, Gin012/Sixième bistrot is now part of Six complex, which includes a design gallery, a hotel and a materials archive. If traditional antipasti with a dash of modern design or vice versa, is the dish of the day, then Gin012/Sixième bistrot is the right location. Inside, diners slouch on velvet cushions, sip sophisticated cocktails and nibble steaks or homemade pasta next to designer lamps. Gin012/Sixième bistrot is beautiful and touches all senses.

Via Scaldasole 7, 20123 Milano
www.sixieme-bistro.com

POTAFIORI

FLOWERS, FOOD, AND MUSIC

Milan has many innovative fusion shops. Potafiori is a fine example, combining a flower shop and bistro, mixing music with good food. The soul of Potafiori are the flowers. They come in all sizes, scents and shape, ready to be transformed into spiral bunches, centre-pieces or bouquets. And while waiting for a floral order, why not enjoy a quick meal, or even stay for an aperitif? Yes, this flower shop is special, and makes Rosalba Picinni, the owner, very proud. Carrying the dream, and combining all Rosalba's passions, this space blossoms from breakfast, through lunch and on to dinner.

Via Salasco 17, 20136 Milano
www.potafiori.com

THE MANZONI

BY TOM DIXON

In May 2019, designer Tom Dixon opened a restaurant and showroom called The Manzoni. True to his motto: "Forget being temporary and build something permanent", the Manzoni is Dixon's first permanent space in continental Europe, giving the brand its own location in Milan. Located close to Milan's La Scala opera house, the stylish restaurant shows furniture and objects designed by the Tom Dixon brand, including a series of upholstered dining and lounge FAT chairs, Melt pendant lamps and Opal translucent globe lights. The shades of classy grey emphasise colourful foods on the plate. As stylish as the interior is the presentation of the dishes.

Via Alessandro Manzoni 5, 20121 Milano
www.themanzoni.com

ROVELLO 18

TRADITION OF GOOD FOOD

Rovello 18 was born from an old family tradition. In 1950 the founder Pierino gave his guests a simple menu of local dishes, always choosing fresh and seasonal ingredients. Rovello was awarded a well-deserved Michelin Star identification. To this day, the dishes at this restaurant are fantastic thanks to these high quality elements. Rovello 18 is recognized as one of the best trattoria in Italy due to the exquisite taste and the great selection of over 800 wines. The interior is typical trattoria style, with walls of heavy wood. It could not be better for a relaxed and cosy night out with family and friends.

Via Tivoli 2, 20121 Milano
www.rovello18.it

28 POSTI

LOVE FOR DETAIL

28 Posti is situated on a side street in the heart of the historic Navigli district. It is a quiet place with only 28 seats. Chef Marco Ambrosino is a true experimenter in the kitchen, and his practice stands out from the common trend. There is no lack of smoked dishes, like seaweed, with flavors of sea urchins and oysters, plankton, powders, aromas and spices. Also on the menu are fermented cabbage, truffle and bergamot. 28 posti is a place to visit with an empty stomach, but more so with an open mind, to analyze, absorb and explore Ambrosino's recipes and combinations.

Via Corsico 1, 20144 Milano
www.28posti.org

CARLO E CAMILLA IN SEGHERIA

DRAMATIC INDUSTRIAL SETTING

What happens if an art director, an exhibitions' curator and a designer start a project? They make magic. Carlo e Camilla in Segheria is a fine restaurant and cocktail bar located in a former factory building. Surrounded by raw concrete walls - the long wooden tables, noble crystal chandeliers and designer seats invite guests to a theatrical-like set. All dishes are served on snow-white porcelain and fuse traditional with modern Italian cuisine. The offer is seasonal and changes 4 times a year, always including meat, fish and vegetarian options with fresh and selected ingredients. The aesthetic and creative culture between Tanja Solci, Carlo Cracco and Nicola Fanti gave birth to Carlo e Camilla.

Via Giuseppe Meda 24, 20141 Milano
www.carloecamillainsegheria.it

AL CORTILE

UNIQUE HISTORICAL ATMOSPHERE

Hidden among warehouses and apartment blocks, this restaurant was established by the head of the Haute cuisine school Food Genius Academy. And although tucked away, it is a magnet for gourmets, and has become one of Milan's most popular meeting points, driven by passionate guests, power women and graduates from the school. The two female chefs are of the most promising on the Milan scene. Their project girls@work support especially women in the industry. The menu offers tapas with typically Italian flavours, from Milan to Rome and back, with mostly fish dishes. Al Cortile awaits from 7pm to 9pm for a tasty aperitif, and until 2am for dinner. After-dinner cocktails are prepared behind a majestic bar counter.

Via Giovenale 7, 20136 Milano
www.alcortile.com

NEBBIA

CREATIVE BISTRO-STYLE DISHES

This modern restaurant is located in the Navigli district, close to the Nuova Accademia di Belle Arti. Nebbia's sophisticated interior is minimalistic and clean. Floors are predominantly in grey tones, whilst walls are supported by pastel-rose curtains and the furniture is wooden. The crockery design is equally minimalistic, allowing one to focus on the presentation of the dishes. Still, Nebbia feels down-to-earth, with humble yet high-quality food. From the Ravioli, to the traditional Polpo (octopus), to the artichoke, every element of food is carefully sourced, and every meal prepared with love. When it comes to wine, the list at Nebbia is long, and perfect to enjoy a Milanese aperitif.

Via Evangelista Torricelli 15, 20136 Milano
www.nebbiamilano.com

VÒCE AIMO E NADIA

CULTURE, ART AND FOOD

Close to the famous Duomo and to La Scala Opera Theater, is this recent addition to Milan's gastronomic culture. VÒCE has been designed as a versatile and multifunctional space - combining the trinity of culture, art and food. It is a cafeteria, a library and above all a fine dining restaurant - all in one. Located within the historic buildings of the Museum of the Gallerie d'Italia, this place entices one to discover architecture, art exhibitions and local delicacies in a unique way. The design reflects the owners' values of elegance, Italian tradition and attention to local products.

Piazza della Scala 6, 20121 Milano
www.voceaimoenadia.com

SAN MAURÍ BISTROT

CREATIVE AND CONTEMPORARY KITCHEN

Eat in an elegant and refined bistro under the shade of the Duomo in the historical center of Milan. San Maurí offers creative and contemporary cuisine with carefully selected ingredients from the region. Whether for lunch or dinner, the dishes are homemade. Popular are the ravioli, the octopus or the Sardinian gnocchi with basil pesto. Antique stone flooring, delicate embellishments on the stucco of the ceilings and old wooden tables emphasize a grand historic feeling while the chefs are preparing the food in an open-plan kitchen. If there is still some space for the dessert, don't miss the tiramisu served in a glass or a light sorbet. It's worth it.

Via S. Maurilio 4, 20121 Milano
www.sanmauri.it

PACIFICO

FLAVOURS FROM SOUTH-AMERICA

Dark blue velvet seats, dim light, shiny chrome and fishes on the walls. Welcome to Pacifico. This restaurant is not under water, but one can imagine being in an elegant submarine. Pacifico is the place in Milan spreading out recipes and flavors from Peruvian-Nikkei cuisine. This dining room offers a fine and intimate atmosphere, attentive service and excellent ingredients. The menu is mainly about seafood - some Nikkei taste, some with a modern Asiatic-fusion twist. An example is the pure sea bass ceviche with leche de tigre, or the mixto, with a larger variety of seafood and a spicy touch. Pacifico invites the curious to immerse themselves for a night in this exotic venue rated on the Micheline guide.

Via della Moscova 29, 20121 Milano
www.wearepacifico.com

DROGHERIA MILANESE

ITALIAN STYLE TAPAS

Invite friends, sit down at a long table in the middle of the bistro, and taste and share Italian-style tapas at La Drogheria. The informal atmosphere is ideal for relaxed brunches or laid-back afternoon coffees in the heart of Milan. La Drogheria brings people together because good food is what everyone shares. Wooden baskets with cutlery, in the middle of the table, encourage you to serve yourself, to feel at home without fuss. A carefully selected wine list completes traditional first and second plates and emphasizes the famous dolce vita in Italy.

Via S. Marco 29, 20121 Milano
www.drogheriamilanese.it

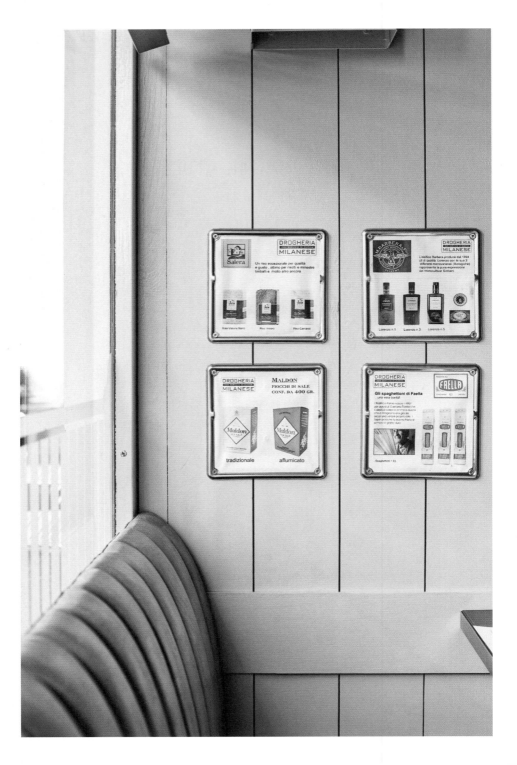

DA ZERO

NEAPOLITAN-STYLE PIZZERIA

The birthplace of pizza is Naples and luckily Milan has an original Neapolitan-style pizzeria located on Via Bernardino Luini. Authentic out-of-the-wooden-oven, thin-crusted, garnished with fresh ingredients and extra-virgin olive oil, and cooked in perfect temperatures. Goodness! Da Zero lures everybody in, willing to share a piece of Italy's culinary history. Even the chef and some waiters are from Napoli, to add that special energy into every pizza. Enjoy an original at Da Zero with colours that reflect the national flag: Tomatoes (red), mozzarella (white), and basil leaves (green): The Pizza Margherita.

Via Bernardino Luini 9, 20123 Milano
www.cominciadazero.com

DRINK

CERESIO 7   137

DOPING CLUB   141

N'OMBRA DE VIN   143

FASHION CAFÉ   145

[LÙ-PO]   147

CERESIO 7

360° VIEW OF THE URBAN SKYLINE

Above the historic Enel building's amazing terrace, rises the Ceresio 7 Restaurant and Pools. Gourmets will enjoy the creations of Chef Elio Sironi at the restaurant and from the bar menu, while taking in the 360° view of the urban skyline. Two swimming pools offer an escape during daytime. Ceresio 7 is a popular place, open all day long - from the morning by the pools, and the lunch on the open-air terrace, to sunset with the typical Aperitivo at the bar, and after-dinner cocktails. A warm and elegant atmosphere accompanies guests while they enjoy a wide and prestigious selection of spirits and drinks. The Bar features two lounges, a smoking room, poolside tables and cabanas.

Via Ceresio 7, 20154 Milano
www.ceresio7.com

DOPING CLUB

AT THE YARD HOTEL

Welcome to luxury little Britain in Milan. The Doping Club at The Yard is a cocktail bar for true gentlemen and lovers of British style - in summer. Leather couches, shelves full of Hendricks Gin, books, art and fashion magazines decorate the seating area. James Bond might be a regular here. A great variety of cocktails and a wide assortment of wines, spirits and liqueurs make this bar perfect for a unique aperitivo. The high-quality cocktails and refined recipes are prepared by mixologist Simone Pappalardo.

Piazza Ventiquattro Maggio, 8, 20123 Milano
www.thedopingclub.com

N'OMBRA DE VIN

APERITIVO BAR

Fancying talking about wine? N'Ombra de Vin is the place. This is the most evocative Aperitivo Bar in Milan. It is a true hotspot for wine and aperitive lovers, as well as younger guests who love to start the evening here. Its location is in the same building as the old 1500's refectory of the Agostinian Friars. Being based next to the Basilica of San Marco makes this wine-bar even more popular. The vaulted ceiling, with columns, walls and floors in stone are the original. N'Ombra is so trendy that often on weekends patrons standing outside block the road. The menu ranges from breakfast, to aperitif, right through to dinner.

Via S. Marco 2, 20121 Milano
www.nombradevin.it

FASHION CAFÉ

REFINED SELECTION OF SPIRITS

The famous and historic district La Brera is the home of Fashion Café. Located in a building designed by Vico Magistretti in the 1950s, this gem is surrounded by galleries, art workshops, and some of the most prestigious design showrooms. Fashion Cafe is an elegant and sophisticated location to unwind. Enjoy it from midday with lunch, until early evening with aperitif and dinner, and after dinner with drinks in the lounge bar. Professional bartenders conjure luxury cocktails inspired by US-American traditions, but with an Italian twist. This warm and elegant setting sparkles to the pace of contemporary life.

Via S. Marco 1, 20121 Milano
www.fashioncafe.it

[LÙ-PO]

BISTRO AND COCKTAIL BAR

When the afternoon sun is softening, and the idea of a well-tempered Campari Orange is growing, then it's time to walk to Via Arese in the Isola district and enjoy an aperitif at Lù-po. This bistro and cocktail bar celebrates the Italian aperitif-culture with gourmet sandwiches, salads and carpaccio. Lù-po is noble, fierce and also warm and welcoming. Colourful vintage bar-stools and an air of classical elegance attract bikers from the neighbourhood, as well as fashion fundis. The Lupo (wolf) parades on the wall as a reference to the logo of El Solitario, a Spanish motorcycle brand belonging to a close friend of the Lù-po owners.

Via Francesco Arese 20, 20159 Milano
www.lupomilano.it

SHOP

ALYSI   151

ATELIER VM   153

TENOHA STORE   155

ANTONIA   157

STAMBERGA   159

FUEGUIA 1833   161

RAW   163

NILUFAR DEPOT   165

ARMANI LIBRI   167

SLAM JAM   169

TEAROSE   171

L'ORTO DI BRERA   173

10 CORSO COMO   175

ALYSI

MODERN, FEMININE AESTHETIC

Whether visiting a modern art exhibition or shopping at a designer boutique, every step in Milan whispers elegance. So too with boutique Alysi, located at Via Ponte Vetero in the historic Brera district. This 130-square-metre store is within a building that dates back to the 1600s. An elegant display of women's clothing fills the entrance. Further inside, the collections are displayed as if an art installation, complementing Alysi's visual style, whilst showcasing various accessories. A dressing room resembles a small lounge - its soft, poised atmosphere features carpets and fixtures that create an intimate environment.

Via Ponte Vetero 6, 20121 Milano
www.alysi.it

ATELIER VM

FINE JEWELLERY

Alchemy is the art of transforming one substance into another. Alchemy is also the power to create something new. At Atelier VM Marta Caffarelli and Viola Naj-Oleari are the experienced alchemists processing metals, stones and other substances into precious jewellery. Rings, bracelets, necklaces or earrings are born here and add beauty to the human body.

The store itself is cosy, made to measure and marked by the neon sign identifying the brand. The marble walls and its colours dominate the space: red jasper, green and honey onyx, blue sodalite and rosa portogallo.

Corso Garibaldi 127, 20121 Milano

www.ateliervm.com

TENOHA STORE

JAPAN MEETS MILAN

Japan meets Milan in the Via Vigevano on 2500 m2. This multifunctional space has created something innovative and comfortable that enriches life every day. Indeed, this is the formula with which Tenoha presents itself on the Milanese scene. Whether clothes, books, gifts or objects, everything in this store is of high quality, functional and beautiful. Everything perfectly displayed. Everything in order. The selection of items in the Tenoha store introduces Japanese values and aesthetics to the Italian market, enriching the lifestyle with new shapes and colours.

Via Vigevano 18, 20144 Milano
www.tenoha.it

ANTONIA

EXCLUSIVE MULTI-BRAND STORE

Located on Via Cusani, in the bustling Brera district, is one of Milan's most successful and exclusive multi-brand stores: Antonia. Here it is easy to get lost among its unique mix of top luxury brands and contemporary streetwear labels, displayed in a unique setting that fuses history and modernity. Antonia offers a lifestyle shopping experience for men and women where Saint Laurent, Valentino, Gucci, Balenciaga, Off-White, Dior, Sacai and Isabel Marant are only a handful of the labels to buy, wear and enjoy. Antonia is much more than a boutique - it is a key reference point for the fashion industry on a global scale. It was founded by Antonia Giacinti and Maurizio Purificato, who still run it today.

Via Cusani 5, 20121 Milano
www.antonia.it

STAMBERGA

CAREFULLY SELECTED PRODUCTS

Located in Milan's design district Porta Venezia, between the Art Deco buildings, and hiding in a quiet courtyard is Stamberga, a multi-brand and multi-category kaleidoscopic space. It bridges East and West, inspiring design, fashion and art lovers all at once. Known as Concept Gallery and Bookseller, Stamberga is also a source of rare-design stationery and Asian style utensils. The selection is eclectic and a good balance of Asian and European utensils. Stamberga started as a photo gallery. Now it offers exclusive objects, from art, to black and white photos, books and magazines, Asian stationary, imported teas and design furniture.

Via Melzo 3, 20129 Milano
www.stamberga.it

FUEGUIA 1833

LIMITED EDITION FRAGRANCES

Bringing Argentina to Italy, in a beautiful flacon full of fragrances, was the idea of Julian Bedel in 2010. Today his perfumery is located in the heart of Milan on Via Tommaso Grossi, with five other branches in major world cities. The ingredients of the perfumes are carefully sourced, and the science of distillation meticulously researched, to design the perfect fragrance for the perfect occasion. Julian Bedel with Fueguia 1833 is also a pioneer in sustainable fragrance production. Sustainability plays a major role in the foundation of the company and in the action it takes. Only certain natural ingredients are used for the first time in perfumery. Fueguia 1833 produces everything in their laboratory in limited-edition quantities of 400 bottles.

Via Tommaso Grossi 1, 20121 Milano
www.fueguia.it

DCW&ditions
PARIS

LAMPE GRAS N. 305

RAW

VINTAGE AND DECOR

Treasure hunters will love Raw, nestled between the beautiful buildings of the historic Milanese center. This cabinet de curiosités – as the sign says - is heaven for vintage and decor lovers. Dive into the rooms of Raw and get lost in furniture, objects and accessories - from the most ancient to the more modern. Every room tells a different story. Raw pays great attention to the smallest details and the curious eye of each customer will be caught by the colours, materials, and shapes. All curiosities are combined in a wide range of products, made by artisans and experts of Italian and international origin.

Via Palermo 1, 20154 Milano
www. rawmilano.it

NILUFAR DEPOT

MILAN'S TOP DESIGN PIECES

Nilufar Depot is worth visiting any time of year, not just during the Milan Design week in April. Because this is the place where Milan's top design pieces can be bought. Nilufar Depot sells vintage, contemporary and 20th-century design pieces. Behind this collection stands Nina Yashar, among the top design dealers on the international scene. She has operated her gallery on Via della Spiga since 1979. In 2015 she opened Nilufar Depot, a massive gallery showcasing her collection of design pieces that she has assembled over the years. Nilufar Depot is a treasure trove and even if one is not looking to buy, Yashar's impeccable collection is sure to inspire.

Viale Vincenzo Lancetti 34, 20158 Milano
www.nilufar.com

ARMANI LIBRI

COLLECTION OF COFFEE TABLE BOOKS

Manzoni 31 has become a legendary address in Milan; the home and headquarters of the Armani empire. And it wouldn't be complete without a bookstore. Inspired by his long friend Walther König and his extensive bookshop in Cologne, Armani proposed that König designs a bookshop for him. He did and Giorgio Armani opened it himself. Minimalist but with attention to detail, intimate and modern, this bookstore represents everything in fashion and design. There is a wall of cult books of the fashion industry. And in the center, a large table with enormous photographic books showing the timeless icons of style.

Via Alessandro Manzoni 31, 20121 Milano
www.buchhandlung-walther-koenig.de

SLAM JAM

MALE STREETWEAR

Find the coolest of the cool outfits for men at Slam Jam.
Located in Brera, right next door to Parco Sempione, Milan's
Slam Jam flagship store is on two levels and has a pop-
up room. Brands like Cav Empt, And Wander, Undercover
can be bought here. And if the shop has a limited-yet-solid
sneaker section, Milanese men storm Slam Jam to get a
piece of the fashion cake. Other pop-up stores are in key
cities, from Paris to New York. Each Slam Jam shop is
dedicated to offering clothing and attitudes from the global
underground, in a space that communicates the lifestyle of
where the product was born.

Via Giovanni Lanza 1, 20121 Milano
www.slamjam.com

TEAROSE

FLORAL AND INTERIOR DECORATION

If not in the heart of the fashion district, where would the most famous multi-brand boutique in Milan be? Here it stands, the elegant and incomparable Tearose Boutique. The fairy-like atmosphere allows the shopper to browse through fashion collections, flowers, fragrances and even furniture. This floral and interior decoration boutique is a temple of beauty, with every square centimeter filled with fifty shades of natural light. Since 1994, when Alessandra Rovati Vitali opened the doors of Tearose, it has attracted aesthetic minds with its refined taste and unmistakable vibrant-yet-delicate touch. Today Tearose is a renowned contemporary trendsetter.

Via Croce Rossa 2, 20121 Milano
www.tearose.it

L'ORTO DI BRERA

FRESHLY PREPARED MEALS

The historic Brera district has always been a favorite place in its history for artists who met, drank and philosophized in bars and literary cafés. Today it is still the same. Brera is a large pedestrian street with restaurants of all price ranges. From the rustic pizzeria to the star restaurant, to after-dinner cocktail bars, it's all here. There're also ice cream parlors, in between boutiques and art shops, street vendors and markets, and amid all this is L'Orto di Brera, a vegetable shop. Probably the most beautiful veggie shop in Milan. Order a freshly prepared meal, and the owner himself will deliver the food by bicycle.

Via S. Carpoforo 6, 20121 Milano
www.ortodibrera.com

10 CORSO COMO

CONCEPT STORE

This is a shopping and dining complex with a galleria - combining outlets that show and sell works of photography, fashion, music, design, cuisine and culture. In fact, Corso Como is a world of its, own exuding art from every corner, terrace and garden, as much in the gallery as in the restaurant. The concept is about presenting the best from A to Z, mixing products and emotions, and opening the mind through every sense. On the ground floor is a bar, a restaurant and the entrance to the store. On the upper level is the photography gallery, the bookshop and the roof garden. An exclusive boutique hotel with 3 rooms shares the same courtyard.

Corso Como 10, 20154 Milano
www.10corsocomo.com

EXPLORE

In the explore category you'll find personally selected galleries and art museums to inspire your stay in Milan - a city filled with spectacular architecture and design exhibitions.
And if you would like to extend your stay with a trip to one of the beautiful lakes, such as Lake Como or Lake Garda, we have included some of our favourite hotels. Here you can relax in one of the most romantic locations in the world.

SPAZIO ROSSANA ORLANDI   179

ARMANI/SILOS   181

MUSEO DEL NOVECENTO   183

FONDAZIONE PRADA   185

IL SERENO LAGO DI COMO   187

FILARIO HOTEL & RESIDENCES   191

LEFAY RESORT SPA LAGO DI GARDA   195

SPAZIO ROSSANA ORLANDI

INFLUENTIAL CURATOR IN THE DESIGN WORLD

Gallerist Rossana Orlandi created a space for vintage contemporary furniture, design, art, books, clothing and accessories. This was once a tie factory and is known today as one of Europe's most important design galleries. What will one find at Rossana Orlandi? Small productions from young cutting-edge designers, unique pieces, limited editions and innovative prototypes. Orlandi also discovers new talent, and gives exposure to newcomers. Top designers like Piet Hein Eek, Maarten Baas, and Nacho Carbonell all received a jump-start from here. Visiting Orlandi's three-story space has become a rite of passage for many - averaging around 30,000 visitors during Milan Design Week.

Via Matteo Bandello 14/16, 20123 Milano
www.rossanaorlandi.com

ARMANI/SILOS

APPEALS TO ALL THE SENSES

Originally a granary, the Armani/Silos is an exhibition space that illustrates Giorgio Armani's professional experience, revealing a rich heritage of unique know-how. Inaugurated in 2015 for the celebrations marking the 40th year of the designer's career, the Silos appeals to all the senses: scent, sound and sight. The permanent collection – showcasing Giorgio Armani's unique creations from 1980 to the present day – is structured around three narrative paths with a selection of approximately 400 outfits and 200 accessories. The space also houses a Digital Archive of sketches, photos and videos on the ready-to-wear and couture collections intended for researchers and fans who want to discover more about the work and style of Giorgio Armani, who personally conceived the renovation project.

Via Bergognone 40, 20144 Milano
www.armani.com/silos

MUSEO DEL NOVECENTO

20TH CENTURY ART

Close to the Duomo, the Museo del Novecento is located right in the city center. It displays approximately four hundred exhibits, most of them Italian, with pieces from national and international artists including Kandinsky, Picasso, Matisse or Modigliani to be admired. Established in 2010 with the goal of spreading knowledge of 20th Century Art, the Museum is also active in the conservation, investigation and promotion of 20th Century Italian cultural and artistic heritage. The museum's bookshop offers gifts to browse whilst one is drinking an espresso. Looking over the Piazza del Duomo from the restaurant-bar rounds off the visit. The Museum also displays temporary exhibitions related to Modern and Contemporary art.

Piazza del Duomo 8, 20123 Milano
www.museodelnovecento.org

FONDAZIONE PRADA

EXQUISITE ART MUSEUM

A four-story house covered with a gold leaf marks the site in the south of the city near the Porta Romana train station. Welcome to Milan's exquisite art museum. A visit is a must, if one wants to truly experience Milan. The Fondazione Prada is located in a former gin distillery built in 1910 and its architecture literally serves art.

Whether it's 'hanging mushrooms from the ceiling' or antiquities, the Fondazione Prada is promoting contemporary art and culture through experimental programs. The art is breathing, and a liberating circulation of images, objects and visitors. The Haunted House itself is magnificent, hosting artworks by Louise Bourgeois and a site specific intervention by Robert Gober.

Largo Isarco 2, 20139 Milano
www.fondazioneprada.org

IL SERENO LAGO DI COMO

NEW ERA OF LUXURY

Just one hour from Milan, in the picturesque town of Torno, along the stunning shores of Lake Como stands this hotel designed by iconic Patricia Urquiola. She created an optical illusion - the hotel seems to float on the water. The interior is sober in colours of green, taupe and blue, while wood finishes give Hotel il Sereno a relaxed feel. Sit by the poolside with a drink – look out onto the lake - this is a perfect spot for an aperitivo. The hotel kitchen is managed by Andrea Berton, who serves Neapolitan dishes touched with buffalo mozzarella, veal tripe and Genovese ragù.

Via Torrazza 10, 22020 Torno CO, Italy
www.ilsereno.com

FILARIO HOTEL & RESIDENCES

A REFRESHING TAKE ON LAKE COMO

Located on the shores of Lake Como, this contemporary design hotel offers quietness, relaxation and body and soul restoration. Once a wire factory, it features modern shapes through glass and stone, with large floor-to-ceiling windows. Light floods the rooms for breathtaking views over the lake. With only thirteen rooms, Filario has an intimate atmosphere, perfect for a romantic break. Decorated in earthy tones, local handmade furniture and textiles, in shades of silky-grey and chocolate-brown, reminds one of the history of Como's districts silk industry. On a hot summer day, a refresher in the infinity pool is a must. It oversees the lake, which is surrounded by mountains. A water taxi can take one anywhere on the lake.

SP583, 89, 22025 Lezzeno CO, Italy
www.filario.it

LEFAY RESORT SPA
LAGO DI GARDA

SPACE, NATURE, SILENCE

Only two hours from Milan, in the picturesque "Riviera dei Limoni" above Gargnano is a pretty town with orange trees. And in a spot with breathtaking views over the Lake Garda stands one of the most innovative and sustainable Spa Resorts in Europe: Lefay.

Combining traditional Chinese medicine with scientific methods, guests can enjoy tailor-made treatments, or choose from a variety of mental and physical wellness packages. Home to one of the best Spas in Italy, Lefay's extensive gardens offer a running circuit, a fitness trail with eight stations and an energy-therapeutic garden. The hotel rooms are several individual buildings embedded so precisely in the slope of the hill, that they hardly can be seen from the lake.

Via Angelo Feltrinelli, 136, 25084 Gargnano BS, Italy
www.lefayresorts.com

10 CORSO COMO	175
28 POSTI	99
AL CORTILE	107
ALYSI	151
ANTONIA	157
ARMANI LIBRI	167
ARMANI/SILOS	181
ATELIER VM	153
CARLO E CAMILLA IN SEGHERIA	103
CERESIO 7	137
DA ZERO	131
DE SANTIS	75
DOPING CLUB	141
DROGHERIA MILANESE	127
FASHION CAFÉ	145
FILARIO HOTEL & RESIDENCES	191
FONDAZIONE PRADA	185
FUEGUIA 1833	161
GIACOMO ROSTICCERIA	77
GINO12/SIXIÈME BISTROT	83
GOD SAVE THE FOOD	61
HOTEL VIU	27
IL SERENO LAGO DI COMO	187
LA LATTERIA	49
LEFAY RESORT SPA LAGO DI GARDA	195
LOCANDA PANDENUS	19
L'ORTO DI BRERA	173
LÙBAR	53
[LÙ-PO]	147

MARCHESI 1824   65

MUSEO DEL NOVECENTO   183

NEBBIA   111

NILUFAR DEPOT   165

N'OMBRA DE VIN   143

oT To   57

PACIFICO   123

PALAZZO SEGRETI   31

PLATO CHIC SUPERFOOD   71

POTAFIORI   87

RAW   163

ROOM MATE BY GIULIA   23

ROVELLO 18   95

SAN MAURÍ BISTROT   119

SLAM JAM   169

SPAZIO ROSSANA ORLANDI   179

STAMBERGA   159

TEAROSE   171

TENOHA   67

TENOHA STORE   155

THE BOTANICAL CLUB   45

THE MANZONI   91

THE SENATO HOTEL   15

THE SISTER HOTEL   39

THE STRAF   35

VÒCE AIMO E NADIA   115

COPYRIGHT

The publisher would like to thank the following for their kind permission to reproduce their photographs:

Erin Wulfsohn (@erinwulfsohn) for Pursch Artistes (@purschartistes) p.7, picture on the bottom; Senato Hotel p. 14-17; Locanda Pandenus p. 18-20; Room Mate by Giulia p.22-24; Hotel Viu p.26-29; Palazzo Segreti p.30-33; The Straf p.34-37; The Sister Hotel, AlbertoStrada p.38-41; Alysi p.150; Atelier VM p.152; Antonia p. 156; FAR Credits Pim Top p. 164; Giovanni Gastel p. 178; Armani Silos - Courtesy of Giorgio Armani p. 180; Mascaroni photos p. 182; Fondazione Prada p. 184; Hotel Il Sereno Lago di Como p. 186-188; Filario Hotel & Residences p. 190-192; Lefay Resort SPA Lago di Garda p. 194-198.

BERLIN

CAPE TOWN

PALMA DE MALLORCA

REYKJAVÍK

PARIS